Hustling and Bustling
BOATS

WHEELS AND AUTOMOBILES

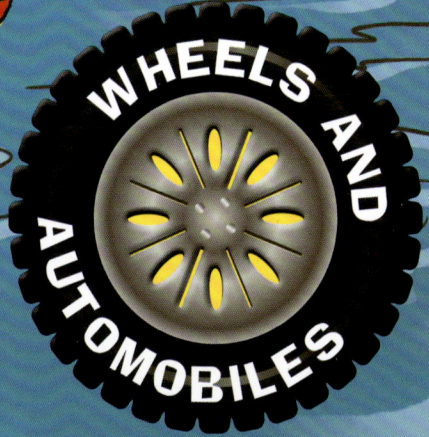

FOX EYE
PUBLISHING

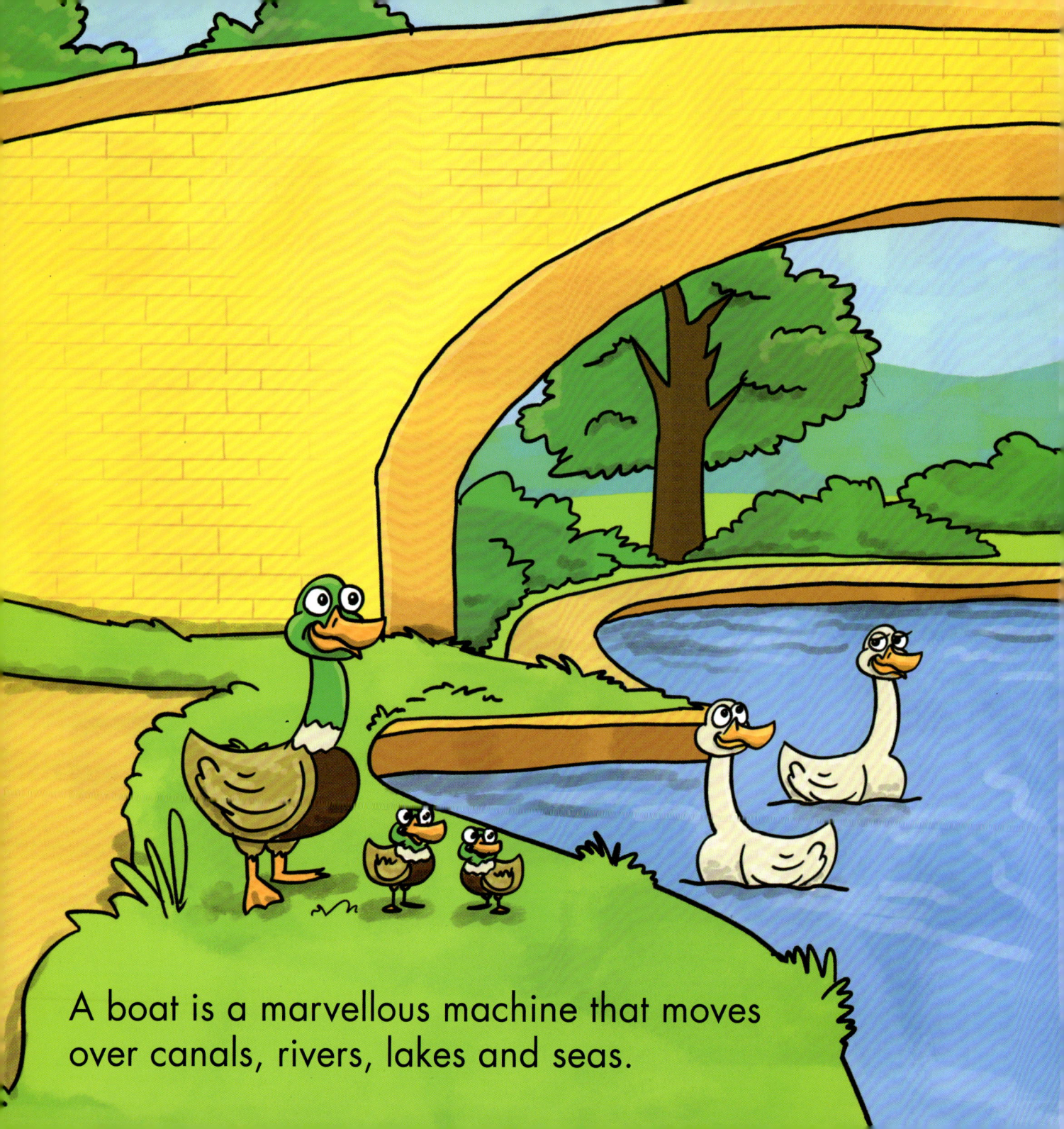

A boat is a marvellous machine that moves over canals, rivers, lakes and seas.

A trip by boat is an amazing adventure
with wonderful things to see.

yacht

houseboat

canal boat

Cargo ships carry heavy loads. Canal boats float, and houseboats are homes. Yachts are fancy. Tugboats pull.

cargo ship

tugboat

dinghy

Submarines dive, and speedboats zoom. Dinghies are dinky. It's fun to play in a little dinghy on the waves.

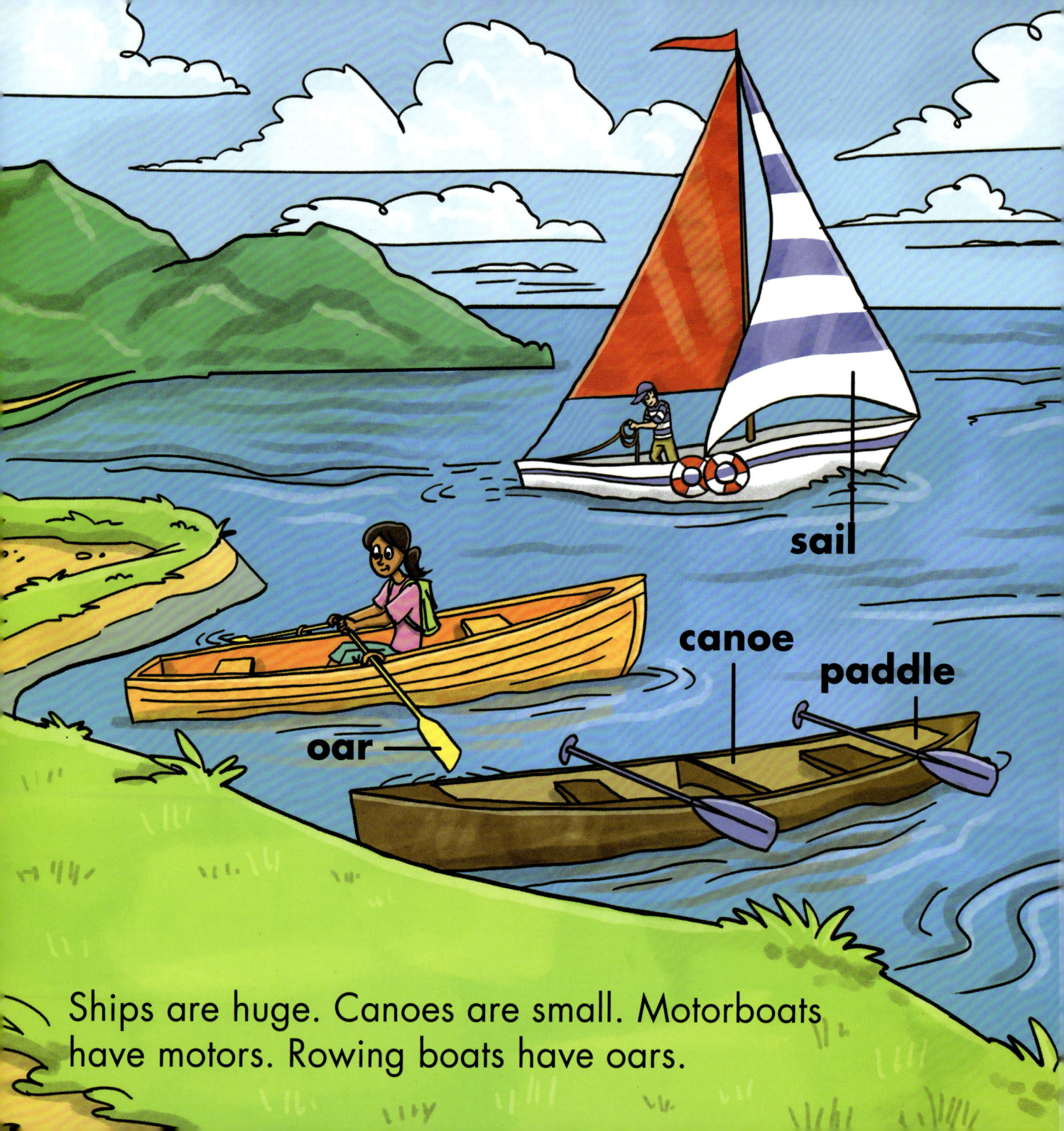

sail

canoe

paddle

oar

Ships are huge. Canoes are small. Motorboats have motors. Rowing boats have oars.

ship

motorboat

Kayaks have paddles. Sailboats have sails.
There are many fine boats in this seafaring tale.

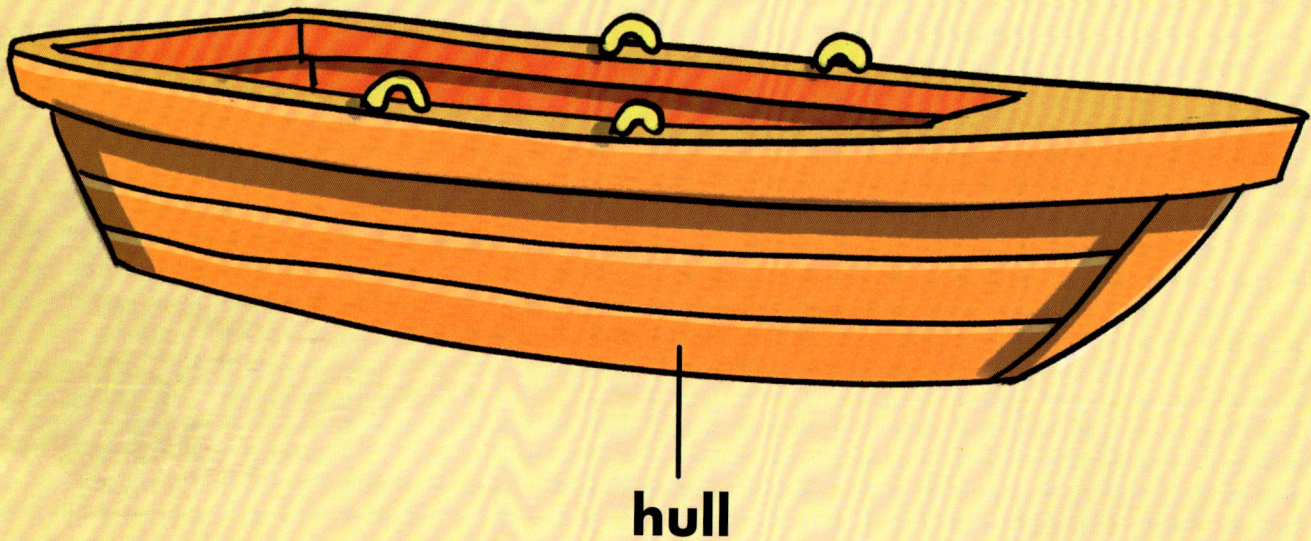

hull

The boat's body is called the hull.
The floor is called the deck.

port

starboard

deck

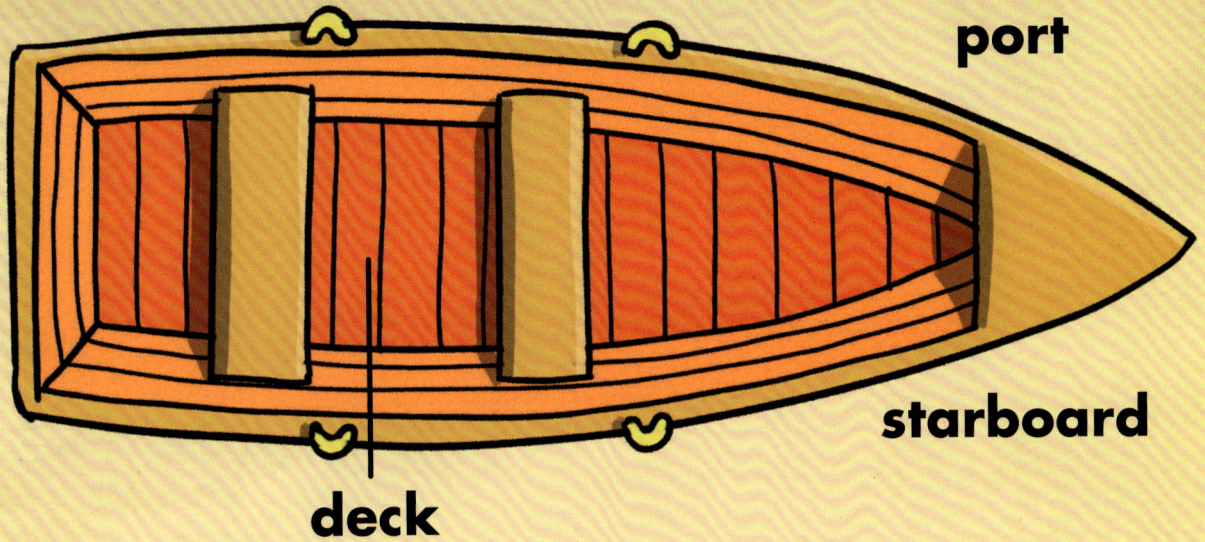

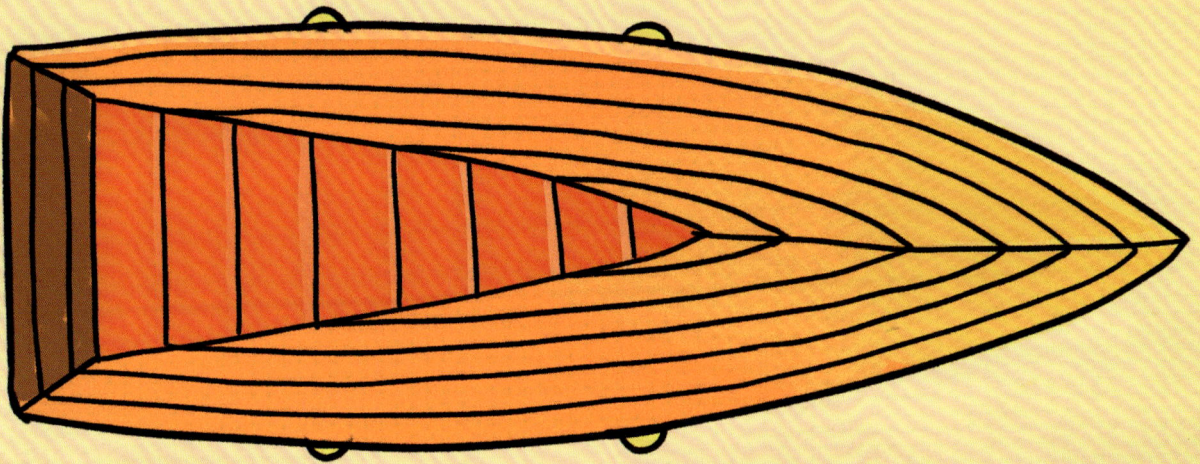

Starboard is on the boat's right side
and port is on the left.

bow

stern

The front of a boat is called the bow.
The back is called the stern. This is where
the rudder is. It helps the boat to turn.

rudder

keel

The keel is underneath the boat. It runs from front to back. It stops the boat from tipping over and landing with a splash.

A motorboat has a motor. It has a propeller, too. The motor turns the propeller around. This helps the boat to move.

propeller

motorboat

This motorboat is a speedboat. It is going very fast. It whizzes over the waves. The dolphins like to chase it. They swim and play in its wake.

rowing boat — — **oar**

First, it passes a rowing boat. It is rowing near the shore. The rowers move the boat by pushing the water with the oars.

The speedboat passes a kayak. It is paddling out to sea. The speedboat heads away from shore. What else shall we see?

sail

mast

sailboat

There goes a shiny sailboat with a sail upon its mast. The sail catches the whistling wind. It makes the boat go fast.

cruise ship

Here comes a mighty cruise ship. It is sailing far from land. The passengers upon the deck smile and wave their hands.

cargo ship

A cargo ship transports many goods in containers from port to port. It signals to others which way it will go with a series of toots from its horn.

submarine

Something moves beneath the boat in waters dark and deep. It rises to the surface. It is a submarine!

Now the sun is going down. The sky is turning red. The speedboat turns back to the shore. It is nearly time for bed.

This watery adventure had boats galore and dolphins in the waves. The little speedboat rests by the shore. Tomorrow's adventure awaits.

Bustling Words

Canals are long, narrow areas of water that have been made by people.

Canoes are small, narrow boats for two people.

A **cruise ship** is a very big ship that takes people to different places for fun.

A **deck** is the surface of the ship that people walk on.

Dolphins are fun-loving sea animals.

Kayaks are small, narrow boats for one or two people.

Lakes are large areas of water that are surrounded by land.

Marvellous means wonderful or amazing.

A **mast** is a tall pole to which a sail is attached.

Motorboats are small boats with a motor, or engine. An engine creates energy for the boat.

Oars are poles with flat blades at either end. They are used by people to make a boat move forwards.

Paddles are poles with flat blades at either end. They are used by people to make a kayak or canoe move forwards.

First published in 2024 by Fox Eye Publishing
Unit 31, Vulcan House Business Centre,
Vulcan Road, Leicester, LE5 3EF
www.foxeyepublishing.com

Author: Katherine Eason
Art director: Paul Phillips
Cover designer: Emma Bailey
Editor: Jenny Rush

All illustrations by Eszter Szepvolgyi

978-1-80445-335-3

Printed in China